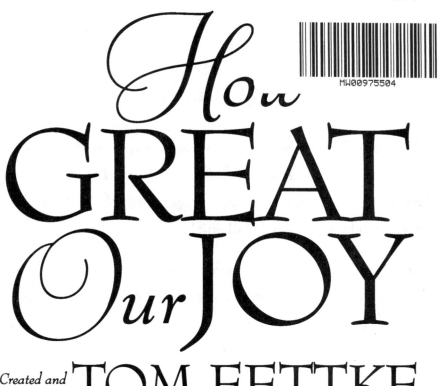

MW00975504

How GREAT Our JOY

Created and Arranged by TOM FETTKE

Orchestrated by Don Marsh, Jim Gray,
Richard Kingsmore, Kyle Hill

Companion Products Available:

Listening Cassette 0-7673-3298-9
(Listening Cassettes available in quantities of ten or more
for $3.00 each from your Music Supplier or Genevox Music Group)

Listening CD 0-7673-3438-8

Accompaniment Cassette 0-7673-3299-7
(Side A Split-track; Side B Instruments only)

Accompaniment CD 0-7673-3300-4
(Split-track only)

Orchestration 0-7673-3301-2
Instrumentation includes: Flute 1-2, Oboe, Clarinet 1-2, Trumpet 1-2-3,
French Horn 1-2-3, Trombone 1-2-3, Tuba, Drum Set, Percussion,
Timpani, Harp, Rhythm, Violin, Viola, Cello, String Bass
Substitute Parts: Alto Sax 1-2-3 (substitute for French Horn 1-2-3),
Tenor Sax/Baritone Treble Clef (substitute for Trombone 1-2),
Clarinet 3 (substitute for Viola), Bass Clarinet (substitute for Cello),
Bassoon (substitute for Cello), Keyboard String Reduction

GENEVOX

Code 0-7673-3297-0

Foreword

With *How Great Our Joy,* Tom Fettke captures the incomparable sense of joy surrounding the birth of Christ. From the orchestral overture to the choral finale, every note of this extraordinary Christmas release shouts "Hallelujah!"

Arranged in chronological order, each section of this innovative work seeks to celebrate the coming of the Messiah as it would have been by those who were there. By Mary, His mother... By the shepherds of the fields... And by the angels from on high.

Yet joy can be expressed in many ways, and *How Great our Joy* integrates them all—combining instrumental passages and narrative sections with a blend of both familiar carols and fresh new compositions.

But perhaps this work's most important element is the opportunity for congregational participation. Like the message that Jesus brought, it is meant to be shared.

Because even as the wise men knelt before His manger, they did not understand the full significance of this event. They could not comprehend that, today when we celebrate the birth of Christ, we find joy in something more.

They could not know ... *How Great Our Joy.*

Sequence

I Opening

Overture and Processional
with
Hallelujah Chorus (from *The Messiah*)

Arranged by Tom Fettke

6

2 Faster ♩ = 104   *"Hallelujah Chorus" (from *The Messiah* —— George Frederick Handel)

8

Lift Up Your Heads

with

Joy to the World

and

Hallelujah Chorus (from *The Messiah*)

Arranged by Tom Fettke

"Lift Up Your Heads" (Steve Fry)

*"Joy to the World" (George Frederick Handel)

14

*"Hallelujah Chorus" (from *The Messiah* – George Frederick Handel)

16

II Mary and Elizabeth

O Magnify

with

Mary's Joy

Arranged by Tom Fettke

*NARRATOR: Mary arose and went into the hill country with haste, to a city of Judah, and entered the house of Zacharias; there she greeted Elizabeth. When Elizabeth heard Mary's greeting the babe leaped in her womb; and Elizabeth was filled with the Holy Spirit. She then spoke out with a loud voice and said:

ELIZABETH (or female narrator): Blessed are you among women, and blessed is the fruit of your womb! Why is this granted to me, that the mother of my Lord should come to me? For indeed, as soon as the voice of your greeting sounded in my ears, the babe leaped in my womb for joy. Blessed is she who has believed that what the Lord has said to her will be accomplished!

NARRATOR: And Mary said:

"Mary's Joy" (Tom Fettke)

Luke 1:39-46 (NKJV altered)

*"O Magnify" (Christopher Machen)

SOLO (Mary)

O, my soul mag - ni - fies,___ mag - ni - fies___ the Lord.___

O, re - joice! My spir - it re - joic - es in God, my Sav - ior.

22

25

30

O Come, O Come, Emmanuel

with

The Advent of Christ

Arranged by Tom Fettke

*NARRATOR 1: The virgin will be with child and will give birth to a son, and they will call Him Immanuel – which means, "God with us."

NARRATOR 2: You who bring good tidings to Zion, go on a high mountain. You who bring good tidings to Jerusalem, lift up your voice with a shout, lift it up, do not be afraid; say to the towns of Judah,

BOTH NARRATORS: "Here is your God!"

Matthew 1:23, Isaiah 40:9 (NIV)

*"The Advent of Christ" (Tom Fettke)

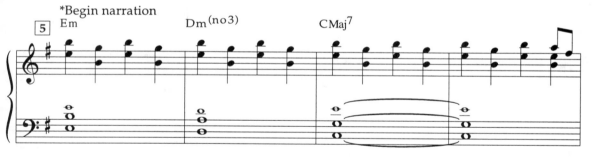

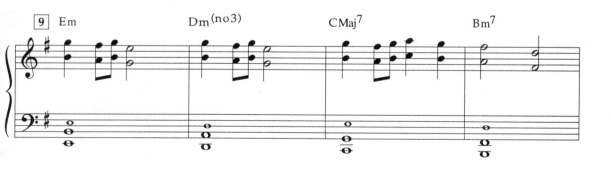

*"O Come, O Come, Emmanuel" (Latin Hymn, translated by John Mason Neale
Plainsong, adapted by Thomas Helmore)

III Bethlehem

A City of the King

JACK COLEMAN

JACK COLEMAN
Edited and arranged by Tom Fettke

40

O Little Town of Bethlehem

with

There Is Hope

and

Thou Didst Leave Thy Throne

Arranged by Tom Fettke

*NARRATOR 2: But you, Bethlehem... out of you will come for me One who will be ruler over Israel. He will stand and shepherd His flock in the strength of the Lord, in the majesty of the name of the Lord His God.

NARRATOR 1: They will live securely, for then His greatness will reach to the ends of the earth. And He will be their peace.

Micah 5:2,4-5 (NIV)

"There Is Hope" (Tom Fettke)

*"O Little Town of Bethlehem"
14 (Phillips Brooks/Lewis H. Redner)

43

*"Thou Didst Leave Thy Throne" (Emily E. S. Elliott/Timothy R. Matthews)

IV The Nativity

Quiet Praise

PENNY SCHAEFFER
and TOM FETTKE

PENNY SCHAEFFER
and TOM FETTKE
Arranged by Tom Fettke

NARRATOR: *(without music)* And Mary brought forth her firstborn Son, and wrapped Him in swaddling clothes, and laid Him in a manger. *(music begins)*

Luke 2:7 (NKJV) altered

O Come, All Ye Faithful

with

For Unto Us a Child Is Born

Arranged by Tom Fettke

*NARRATOR 1: For unto us a Child is born,

NARRATOR 2: Unto us a Son is given:

NARRATOR 1: And the government shall be upon His shoulders:

NARRATOR 2: And His name shall be called Wonderful Counsellor,

NARRATOR 1: The mighty God,

NARRATOR 2: The everlasting Father,

BOTH NARRATORS: The Prince of Peace.

Isaiah 9:6 (KJV)

"For Unto Us a Child Is Born" (from *The Messiah* – George Frederick Handel)

*"O Come, All Ye Faithful" (Latin Hymn, translated by Frederick Oakley/John Francis Wade)

56

V Angels

Glory to God in the Highest

Text Adaptation by
RICHARD KINGSMORE

RICHARD KINGSMORE
Arranged by Tom Fettke

*NARRATOR: When the angels had left them and gone into heaven, the shepherds said to one another, "Let's go to Bethlehem and see this thing that has happened, which the Lord has told us about."

Luke 2:15 (NIV)

Angels We Have Heard on High

with

Angels, from the Realms of Glory

Arranged by Tom Fettke

"Angels We Have Heard on High"
(Traditional French Carol/Traditional French Melody)

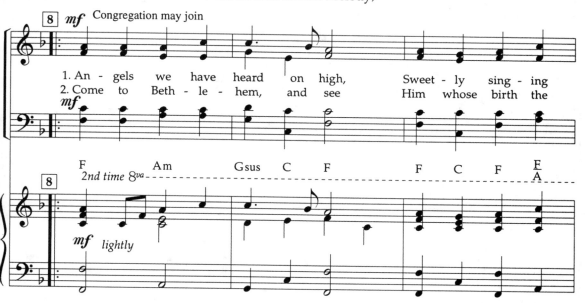

1. An - gels we have heard on high, Sweet - ly sing - ing
2. Come to Beth - le - hem, and see Him whose birth the

70

72

74

VI Shepherds

Gonna See a Baby

AL VINCENT

ROBERT BROWN
Arranged by Tom Fettke

78

80

Sent His Son, Je - sus, sent His Son, Je - sus,

G   Am⁷   G   Am⁷

Sent His Son, Je - sus, to show His love.

G   Am⁷   Bm⁷   Am⁷   C/D   G   Dm⁷   FMaj⁷

G   FMaj⁷   G/D   G   Gsus/D   G

How Great Our Joy

TRADITIONAL GERMAN CAROL

TRADITIONAL GERMAN MELODY
Arranged by Tom Fettke

*NARRATOR 1: And the shepherds came with haste and found Mary and Joseph, and the Babe lying in a manger.

NARRATOR 2: Now when they had seen Him, they made widely known the saying which was told them concerning this Child.

NARRATOR 1: And all those who heard it marveled at those things which were told to them by the shepherds.

NARRATOR 2: But Mary kept all these things and pondered them in her heart.

NARRATOR 1: Then the shepherds returned, glorifying and praising God for all the things that they had heard and seen.

Luke 2:16-20 (NKJV)

84

Congregation may join

1. While by the sheep we watched_ at night, Glad ti-dings brought an

85

2. There shall the Child lie in a stall, This Child who shall re-deem us all. How great our joy! Great our joy! Joy, joy, joy! Joy, joy, joy! Praise we the Lord in

88

VII Magi

Thus Was He Born
A Cappella
or accompanied by keyboards

JACK COLEMAN

JACK COLEMAN
Arranged by Tom Fettke

*If orchestral tape tracks are being used, this accompaniment should be played by a live instrument or instruments. A guide track is <u>not</u> provided on the accompaniment products.

Low - ly — and hum - bly the Lord was born. A star was His sign and God's love was the rea - son He came for man -

18
a tempo
decresc. poco a poco
ff
kind.
Ah
ff
18
a tempo
decresc. poco a poco
ff
rit.
D. S. al Coda
D. S. al Coda
rit.
CODA
mp
came
for
man
-
kind.
mp
CODA
mp

Jacob's Star

MICHAEL CARD

SCOTT BRASHER
Arranged by Tom Fettke

NARRATOR 2: *(without music)* A star went ahead of the Magi until it stopped over the place where the Child was. *(music begins)* When they saw the star they were overjoyed.

NARRATOR 1: On coming to the house, they saw the Child with His mother Mary, and they bowed down and worshiped Him. Then they opened their treasures and presented Him with gifts of gold and of frankincense and of myrrh.

Matthew 2:9-11 (NIV altered and abridged)

94

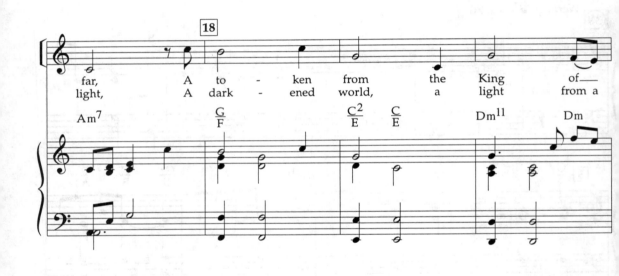

VIII Finale

Hark! The Herald Angels Sing
with
He Is Born

Arranged by Tom Fettke

(Narration begins at measure 11)

*NARRATOR 1: Arise, shine, for your light is come and the glory of the Lord rises upon you.

NARRATOR 2: Nations will come to your light, and kings to the brightness of your dawn.

Isaiah 60:1,3 (NIV)

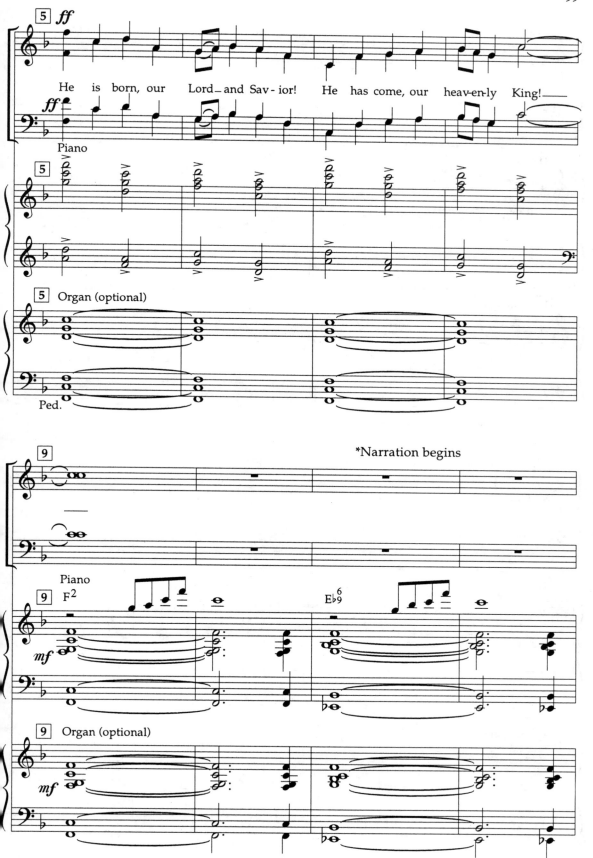

He is born, our Lord— and Sav - ior! He has come, our heav-en-ly King!—

Piano

Organ (optional)

Ped.

*Narration begins

Piano

F^2

$E\flat^6_9$

Organ (optional)

100

*"Hark! The Herald Angels Sing" (Charles Wesley/Felix Mendelssohn)

1st verse: unison melody throughout
2nd verse: parts

103

*"He Is Born" (Jimmy Owens)

*© Copyright 1980 Bud John Songs (ASCAP). Adm. by EMI Christian Music Publishing.

106

Born to bear the sin— of— man - y, Born to— give— e - ter - nal— life.

He shall rule with righ - teous judg - ment O - ver all the

108

How Great Our Joy Congregational Word Sheet

Joy to the World
Joy to the world! the Lord is come;
Let earth receive her King;
Let ev'ry heart prepare Him room
And heav'n and nature sing,
And heav'n and nature sing,
An heav'n, and heav'n and nature sing.

Joy to the earth! the Savior reigns;
Let men their songs employ;
While fields and floods,
rocks, hills, and plains
Repeat the sounding joy,
Repeat the sounding joy,
Repeat, repeat the sounding joy.

Hallelujah Chorus
King of kings! and Lord of lords!
King of kings! and Lord of lords!
And He shall reign for ever and ever,
King of kings! and Lord of lords!
Hallelujah! Hallelujah!
Hallelujah! Hallelujah!
Hallelujah!

O Come, O Come, Emmanuel
O come, O come, Emmanuel,
And ransom captive Israel,
That mourns in lonely exile here,
Until the Son of God appear.

Rejoice! Rejoice! Emmanuel
Shall come to thee, O Israel!

O come, Thou Dayspring, come and cheer
Our spirits by Thine advent here;
And drive away the shades of night,
And pierce the clouds and bring us light!

Rejoice! Rejoice! Emmanuel
Shall come to thee, O Israel!

O Little Town of Bethlehem
O little town of Bethlehem,
How still we see thee lie!
Above thy deep and dreamless sleep
The silent stars go by;
Yet in thy dark streets shineth
The everlasting Light;
The hopes and fears of all the years
Are met in thee tonight.

How silently, how silently
The wondrous gift is giv'n!
So God imparts to human hearts
The blessings of His heav'n.
No ear may hear His coming,
But in this world of sin,
Where meek souls will receive Him, still
The dear Christ enters in.

Angels We Have Heard on High
Angels we have heard on high,
Sweetly singing o'er the plains:
And the mountains in reply,
Echo back their joyous strains.

Gloria in excelsis Deo!
Gloria in excelsis Deo!

Come to Bethlehem, and see
Him whose birth the angels sing;
Come, adore on bended knee
Christ the Lord, the newborn King.

Gloria in excelsis Deo!
Gloria in excelsis Deo!

How Great Our Joy
While by the sheep we watched at night,
Glad tidings brought an angel bright.

How great our joy! Great our joy!
Joy, joy joy! Joy, joy, joy!
Praise we the Lord in heav'n on high!
Praise we the Lord in heav'n' on high!

There shall the Child lie in a stall,
This Child who shall redeem us all.

How great our joy! Great our joy!
Joy, joy joy! Joy, joy, joy!
Praise we the Lord in heav'n on high!
Praise we the Lord in heav'n' on high!

This gift of God we'll cherish well,
That ever joy our hearts shall fill.

How great our joy! Great our joy!
Joy, joy joy! Joy, joy, joy!
Praise we the Lord in heav'n on high!
Praise we the Lord in heav'n' on high!

Hark! The Herald Angels Sing
Hark! the herald angels sing,
"Glory to the newborn King;
Peace on earth and mercy mild;
God and sinners reconciled!"
Joyful, all ye nations, rise,
Join the triumph of the skies;
With the angelic host proclaim,
"Christ is born in Bethlehem!"
Hark! the herald angels sing,
"Glory to the newborn King."

Hail the heav'nborn Prince of Peace!
Hail the Sun of righteousness!
Light and life to all He brings,
Ris'n with healing in His wings.
Mild He lays His glory by,
Born that man no more may die,
Born to raise the sons of earth,
Born to give them second birth.
Hark! the herald angels sing,
"Glory to the newborn King."